W9-BJP-554

THE NBA

A HISTORY OF HOOPS

Published by Creative Education
P.O. Box 227, Mankato, Minnesota 56002
Creative Education is an imprint of The Creative Company
www.thecreativecompany.us

Design and production by Christine Vanderbeek
Art direction by Rita Marshall

Printed by Corporate Graphics in the United States of America

Photographs by Corbis (Bettmann), Dreamstime (Munktcu), Getty Images
(Bill Baptist/NBAE, Nathaniel S. Butler/NBAE, Ned Dishman/NBAE, D. Clarke
Evans/NBAE, Focus On Sport, Jonathan Hodson, Walter Iooss Jr./Sports
Illustrated, Mitchell Layton/NBAE, Vito Palmisano, Doug Pensinger, Dick
Raphael/NBAE, SM/AIUEO, Murat Taner, Tony Triolo/Sports Illustrated,
Jerry Wachter/NBAE), iStockphoto (Brandon Laufenberg)

Library of Congress Cataloging-in-Publication Data
Silverman, Steve.
The story of the Washington Wizards / by Steve Silverman.
p. cm. — (The NBA: a history of hoops)
Includes index.
Summary: The history of the Washington Wizards professional basketball
team from its start as the Chicago Packers in 1961 to today, spotlighting the
franchise's greatest players and moments.
ISBN 978-1-58341-965-6
1. Washington Wizards (Basketball team)—History—Juvenile literature.
2. Washington Bullets (Basketball team)—History—Juvenile literature.
3. Basketball—Washington (D.C.)—History—Juvenile literature. I. Title. II. Series.
GV885.52.W37S55 2010   796.323'6409753—dc22   2009036121

CPSIA: 120109 PO1093

First Edition
2 4 6 8 9 7 5 3 1

Page 3: Forward Caron Butler
Pages 4–5: 2008 playoffs pregame at the Verizon Center

THE STORY OF THE
WASHINGTON
WIZARDS

STEVE SILVERMAN

CREATIVE EDUCATION

CONTENTS

CHAPTER ONE

THE BULLETS BEGIN

As America's capital, Washington, D.C., is the center of the United States' government. The White House is home to the president, the Capitol is home to the House of Representatives and the Senate, and the U.S. Supreme Court rules on the nation's laws. Thousands of tourists travel to Washington every year to visit the Smithsonian Institution, the Washington Monument, and the Lincoln Memorial, and to watch the production of money at the Bureau of Engraving and Printing.

Washington is more than just a hotbed of politics and tourism, though. Washingtonians are also wild about sports, and the nation's capital is home to teams in all four major professional leagues: baseball's Nationals, hockey's Capitals, football's Redskins, and, since 1963, the National Basketball Association's (NBA) Wizards. The Wizards did not originate in Washington, though. They have their roots not on the East Coast but in the Midwest.

Washington, commonly referred to as simply "D.C.," boasts some of America's most spectacular structures, including the U.S. Capitol.

The Wizards were born in Chicago, Illinois, in 1961 as an NBA expansion franchise called the Packers. The Packers (who changed their name to Zephyrs just a year later) took the typical expansion team lumps, going just 18–62. They proved a little more competitive in their second season, going 25–55, thanks largely to the leadership and slick passing of veteran guard Si Green, and yet basketball fans in Chicago seemed disinterested in the franchise.

Prompted by sagging fan support, the team moved to Baltimore, Maryland, prior to the 1963–64 season and was renamed yet again, becoming the Bullets. The club struggled for wins in its first two seasons in Baltimore, yet the Bullets showed signs of feistiness. In the final game of the 1963–64 season, Baltimore notched a 108–95 win over the powerhouse Boston Celtics, who would go on to win the NBA championship.

The Bullets featured mediocre guard play during those early years, but their front line of center Walt "Big Bells" Bellamy and forwards Terry Dischinger and Gus Johnson formed an imposing trio that regularly punished opponents with physical play. Bellamy offered sheer size and a balanced low-post game, while Dischinger was a prime-time scorer.

The 6-foot-6 Johnson, meanwhile, earned a reputation as one of the game's tough guys. "I went up against a lot of the toughest and most competitive forwards and centers in the NBA, and none were tougher than Gus Johnson," San Francisco Warriors center Nate Thurmond later said. "I had to go up against Wilt Chamberlain and Bill Russell, so I knew who the toughest players were in the game. Johnson would fight you for every rebound, for every loose ball, and never give an inch. At the time, Johnson was the best all-round forward in the league, bar none. A couple of more inches in height, and he would have been unstoppable."

In 1964, the Bullets traded Dischinger, guard Rod Thorn, and forward Don Kojis to the Detroit Pistons for a package of five players that included forward Bailey Howell and guards Don Ohl and Wally Jones. Howell and Ohl, the centerpieces of the swap, were smart players who always

WALT BELLAMY WAS THE CORNER-STONE OF THE CHICAGO PACKERS/ZEPHYRS FRANCHISE AND RE-MAINED SO UPON ITS MOVE TO BALTIMORE. Bellamy was the franchise's top overall draft pick in 1961. The former Indiana University standout was a powerful player, but his surprising finesse and footwork around the basket were his greatest assets. Bellamy charged out of the gates by averaging 31.6 points and 19 rebounds as a rookie. He continued to excel after that, averaging 26.8 points and 16.6 boards per game during his 5 seasons with the team, and he did it with a smooth and unhurried style. Still, few fans considered "Big Bells" to be in the same class as great centers of the era such as Wilt Chamberlain, Bill Russell, and Willis Reed. To some, his style could be a little *too* unhurried. Former Zephyrs/Bullets coach Bobby "Slick" Leonard admired Bellamy's talent but always wanted just a bit more from the star. "Walt wasn't a highly motivated player night in and night out," said Leonard. "He'd have some great games, and then he'd have one where he [mentally] didn't show up. But he was an excellent player."

INTRODUCING...

WALT BELLAMY

POSITION CENTER
HEIGHT 6-FOOT-11
PACKERS / ZEPHYRS / BULLETS
SEASONS 1961–66

seemed to be at their best during clutch situations. This new talent helped

the 1964–65 Bullets go 37–43 and claim a spot in the Western Division

playoffs. The scrappy team from Baltimore shocked the St. Louis Hawks,

beating them in the first round, then played the mighty Los Angeles Lak-

ers tough in the Western Division finals before losing, four games to two.

The Bullets appeared ready to build upon that success the following

year, but an inexplicable trade with the New York Knicks put them in

an early hole. Baltimore sputtered after swapping Bellamy for high-

jumping forward Johnny Green and guards Johnny Egan and Jim "Bad

News" Barnes. The team bounced back to make the playoffs, but the

Hawks then gained a measure of postseason revenge, sweeping the

Bullets in three games.

The 1966–67 season was a disastrous one for Baltimore, which

struggled to score and could muster only a 20–61 record. Fortunately,

help was coming, for in the 1967 NBA Draft, the Bullets used the second

overall pick to select a sensational point guard from Winston-Salem State

University named Earl Monroe.

CHAPTER TWO

THE PEARL
SETS THE PACE

Nicknamed "The Pearl," Earl Monroe was one of the speedi-est and flashiest point guards the NBA had ever seen, and he wasted no time in becoming a star. As a rookie, he poured in an average of 24.3 points per game and thrilled Baltimore fans with his array of spin moves, tantalizingly high-bouncing dribble, soaring shots, and slick passes to his team-mates. That cast of teammates improved dramatically in 1968 when the Bullets drafted powerful center Wes Unseld. With Monroe at the point and Unseld down low, the Bullets almost instantly morphed from a hustling but struggling team into a dominant one, going 57–25 in 1968–69.

The Knicks swept Baltimore out of the 1969 playoffs, but Monroe later recalled 1968–69 as the season the Bullets came of age. "The thing that I remember is really turning the corner that year," he said. "When we got Wes, we really got much better. There were games that were very close that we

Playing alongside Earl Monroe, reliable forward Leroy Ellis (pictured) had a key role in the Bullets' turnaround in the seasons of the late 1960s.

probably would have lost in a previous year, but we started winning those games. I remember how a tip-in by Gus [Johnson] or a tip-in by Wes would win us games. Those guys gave us a tremendous edge on the boards, and it seemed like we got all the important rebounds. I think that gave us the impetus to know that we could win in this league."

If Monroe was Baltimore's spark, then Unseld was its backbone. Although Unseld stood only 6-foot-7, his extraordinary strength compensated for his lack of height when battling the NBA's biggest centers. Once Unseld positioned himself near the hoop, opposing players simply could not move him. The stout center's ability to gather in rebounds and quickly send strong, overhead outlet passes to Monroe and guards Kevin Loughery and Jack Marin became a staple of the Bullets' game plan, giving Baltimore a fearsome fast-break attack.

In 1969–70, the Bullets went 50–32, then drew the Knicks again in the playoffs. New York was loaded with talented players that year, including guard Walt Frazier and center Willis Reed, but Bullets coach Gene Shue countered with his own dynamic guard-center duo of Monroe and Unseld. The series played out as an exciting slugfest, but New York ultimately used its home-court advantage to win in seven games.

COURTSIDE STORIES

BULLETS VERSUS KNICKS

Gus Johnson scores against New York.

THE BALTIMORE BULLETS BECAME A CONTENDER WHEN THEY DRAFTED GUARD EARL MONROE AND CENTER WES UNSELD. NBA fans were treated to some memorable springtime moments from 1969 to 1974, when the Bullets and Knicks met in the playoffs for six consecutive years. The Knicks won five of the six playoff series, but that apparent domination does not tell the whole story. The Bullets forced the Knicks to a Game 7 in the 1970 playoffs, the season New York won its first NBA title. The defending champs then got dethroned by the Bullets in Game 7 the following year. Since the final game was in New York, many fans assumed a Knicks victory. Monroe and Unseld would have none of it, though, leading the Bullets through a nasty, physical contest to a 93–91 win. "It was as good a moment as a player could have," Monroe recalled. "We went into Madison Square Garden, and we beat the NBA champions in the seventh game. It was a close game, but we were the better team."

KNOWN AS "THE PEARL" FOR HIS DAZZLING PLAY AND "BLACK MAGIC" FOR HIS PHENOMENAL BALL HANDLING, EARL MONROE WAS ONE OF THE MOST SPECTACULARLY ENTERTAINING PLAYERS IN NBA HISTORY. Monroe was a dominant scorer with the Bullets and won the 1968 NBA Rookie of the Year award when he came out of tiny Winston-Salem State University and averaged 24.3 points and 4.3 assists per game. More than just statistics, though, it was the way the Pearl played that opened eyes around the league. In addition to making the basketball look like a yo-yo when it was in his control, Monroe was able to consistently get good shots down low despite venturing into the neighborhood of towering centers. His secret lay in the uncanny ability to leap high and hang in mid-air, seemingly in order to buy time and get a better release on his shot. "The thing is, I don't know what I'm going to do with the ball," Monroe once said in explaining his offensive success. "If I don't know, I'm quite sure the guy guarding me doesn't know either."

INTRODUCING...

EARL MONROE

POSITION GUARD
HEIGHT 6-FOOT-3
BULLETS SEASONS 1967–72

WES UNSELD'S HEIGHT WAS NO MISPRINT. He manned the Bullets' center position for 13 years despite standing just 6-foot-7. High-school teams can often get by with a center of that height, but not good college teams, and certainly not NBA teams. But while Unseld lacked height, he had an overabundance of strength. He was a 245-pound bull who was fearless when defending the lane or going after rebounds. Besides his power, Unseld's calling card was his ability to grab defensive rebounds and then send two-handed, overhead outlet passes down-court to start Washington fast breaks. The Bullets became a winning team as soon as they drafted Unseld out of the University of Louisville in 1968. They finished his rookie year 57–25, and Unseld averaged 13.8 points and a jaw-dropping 18.2 rebounds per game to earn not only Rookie of the Year honors but the NBA Most Valuable Player (MVP) award as well. "He was a presence on the court," said Bullets guard Earl Monroe. "He may have been a quiet individual, but he made his presence felt."

INTRODUCING...

WES UNSELD

POSITION CENTER
HEIGHT 6-FOOT-7
BULLETS SEASONS 1968–81

By the start of the 1970–71 season, the Bullets were a mature and determined team. They went a disappointing 42–40 but increased their efforts in the playoffs, knocking off the Philadelphia 76ers to earn yet another date with the hated Knicks. The series was another classic, as the teams again split the first six games. But the determined Bullets refused to lose this time, going into New York's Madison Square Garden and winning Game 7 by a score of 93–91.

With that satisfying victory, the Bullets found themselves in the NBA Finals, facing a tough Milwaukee Bucks team that was led by two legendary players: center Lew Alcindor (later named Kareem Abdul-Jabbar) and guard Oscar Robertson. The Bullets had no answers for the towering Alcindor, and the Bucks rolled to a four-game sweep.

Bullets management shocked and outraged many Baltimore fans in 1971 when they traded Monroe to the Knicks in a move that brought swingman Mike Riordan and forward Dave Stallworth to town. While Riordan would become an excellent player for the Bullets, the Knicks seemed to get the better end of the swap. The two teams met in the playoffs each of the next three seasons, and New York beat Baltimore every time.

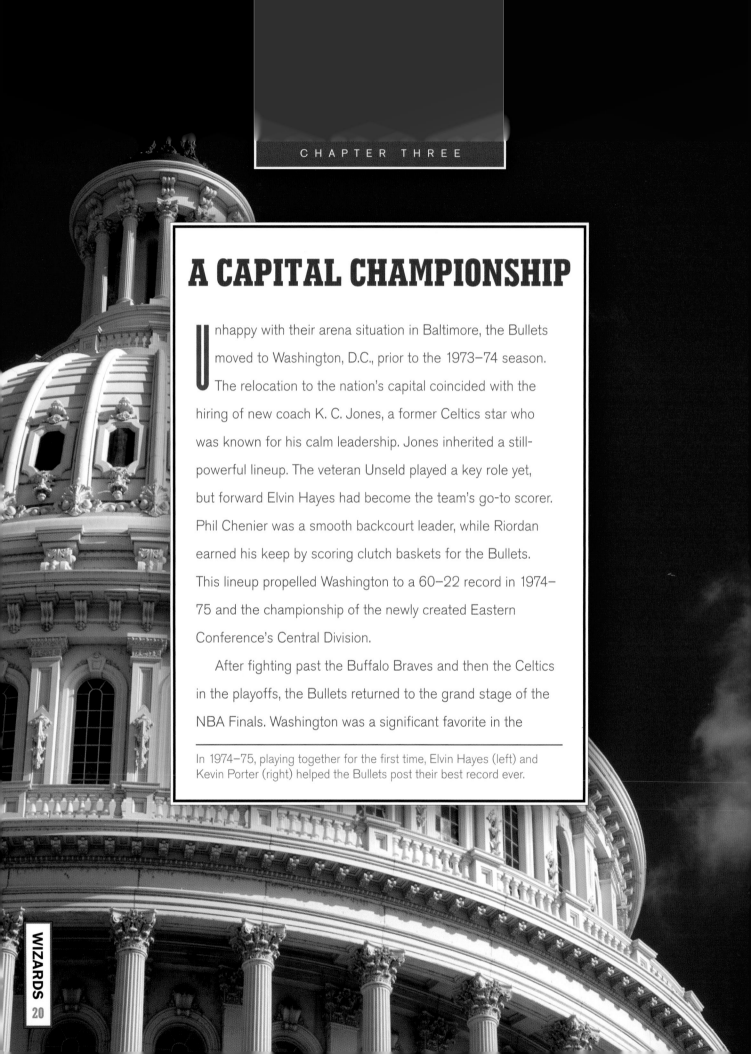

CHAPTER THREE

A CAPITAL CHAMPIONSHIP

Unhappy with their arena situation in Baltimore, the Bullets moved to Washington, D.C., prior to the 1973–74 season. The relocation to the nation's capital coincided with the hiring of new coach K. C. Jones, a former Celtics star who was known for his calm leadership. Jones inherited a still-powerful lineup. The veteran Unseld played a key role yet, but forward Elvin Hayes had become the team's go-to scorer. Phil Chenier was a smooth backcourt leader, while Riordan earned his keep by scoring clutch baskets for the Bullets. This lineup propelled Washington to a 60–22 record in 1974–75 and the championship of the newly created Eastern Conference's Central Division.

After fighting past the Buffalo Braves and then the Celtics in the playoffs, the Bullets returned to the grand stage of the NBA Finals. Washington was a significant favorite in the

In 1974–75, playing together for the first time, Elvin Hayes (left) and Kevin Porter (right) helped the Bullets post their best record ever.

THE 1974–75 WASHINGTON BULLETS WERE ONE OF THE BEST TEAMS IN NBA HISTORY NEVER TO WIN AN NBA TITLE, AS THEY WERE STUNNED IN THE 1975 FINALS BY THE GOLDEN STATE WARRIORS AFTER PUTTING TOGETHER A 60–22 RECORD. While the team fell short of its ultimate goal, the Bullets treated their home fans to a record of success that season that has never again been seen in Washington. The Bullets won 22 straight games at home in the Capital Centre between November 27, 1974, and March 5, 1975. Coached by K. C. Jones and led by explosive forward Elvin Hayes and sharpshooting guard Phil Chenier, the Bullets won 16 of those games by 10 or more points and 11 games by 15 or more. The streak came to an end March 9 in a 113–110 loss to the Philadelphia 76ers, but the Bullets resumed their home dominance by winning seven of their next eight regular-season home games. "We were in the comfort zone when we played at the Capital Centre," Chenier said. "We felt like we could shoot well there, and our confidence level was high."

COURTSIDE STORIES
HOME COOKING

K. C. Jones watches his team from the bench during a 1974 game.

Finals versus the upstart Golden State Warriors, who featured forward Rick Barry but few other big stars. In an incredible upset, the Warriors stunned the Bullets, winning four closely contested games and sweeping the series. "It was very hard to take considering how hard we had worked to get to the Finals," Hayes later said. "I'm not taking anything away from the Warriors, because they were a very good team and very competitive. But there was nobody in our locker room who wouldn't have wanted another shot at them. Let's face it: we thought we were better than they were."

ELVIN HAYES WAS AS ENIGMATIC AS HE WAS TALENTED. The explosive forward proved to be the ideal complement to center Wes Unseld in the front-court, but he had developed a reputation as a testy and hard-to-coach player prior to being traded to Baltimore in 1972. "The Big E" had not gotten along with the coaching staff as a member of the San Diego (and later, Houston) Rockets, and many people thought Baltimore coach Gene Shue would not be able to handle his volatile personality. But Hayes committed himself to basketball excellence while with the Bullets and proved a dynamic all-around threat. He averaged 21.3 points and 12.7 rebounds per game during his 10 years with the Bullets and was even more dangerous in the playoffs.

He was the single most dominant player during the Bullets' run to the 1978 NBA championship, and winning the title was the most satisfying moment of Hayes's career. "Finally winning the championship completes the picture," the forward said. "Because no one can ever again say that E's not a champion."

The Bullets' run of playoff heartbreak finally came to an end in 1978. The team was starting to show its age, but behind Hayes and such players as forwards Bob Dandridge and Kevin Grevey, Washington still had the potential to put huge numbers on the scoreboard. The team played well enough in the 1977–78 regular season, going 44–38, but few fans or sportswriters thought the Bullets had a championship run in them. However, Dick Motta—who had replaced Jones as head coach the year before—ratcheted up the intensity as the playoffs began, demanding that every one of his players put a full effort on the floor.

The Bullets beat the Hawks, San Antonio Spurs, and 76ers in the Eastern Conference playoffs, leaving just one opponent—the Seattle SuperSonics—between them and their first NBA championship. The SuperSonics grabbed a three-games-to-two lead in the Finals. But Hayes, Unseld, and the rest of the Bullets would not be denied this time, crushing Seattle by 35 points in Game 6 and then managing

a 105–99 win on the road in Game 7. Washington finally had its title. "This is why we hung together and worked so hard," said a joyous Hayes. "It was all worth it. From the pain of losing to Golden State to winning the title. That's why you play the game, and it was even better than you thought it would be."

Washington marched right back to the NBA Finals the next year, again meeting Seattle. This time, though, fate favored the Sonics, who triumphed in five games. Bullets fans didn't know it yet, but that was to be the team's last hurrah. As a new decade began, Washington slid into a long run of mediocrity.

CHAPTER FOUR

DRY TIMES
AND A REBIRTH

The Bullets' lineup was reconfigured in the early 1980s as veterans such as Hayes and Unseld were traded away or retired. Two new arrivals ensured that, even if Washington's talent level dropped, its reputation for physical play would remain intact. Those players were center/forwards Jeff Ruland and Rick Mahorn, a pair of hardworking widebodies who often seemed to want to prove their toughness nearly as much as they wanted to win games. Ruland showed a fine scoring touch as he averaged nearly 19 points a game from 1982–83 through 1985–86. Mahorn, meanwhile, averaged nearly 10 boards a game in 1982–83 and 1983–84.

Jeff Ruland's size (6-foot-11 and 280 pounds) made him an intimidator but also contributed to foot injuries that shortened his career.

While many Washington fans loved their so-called "Bruise Brothers," many opponents saw them as thugs. Hall of Fame Celtics announcer Johnny Most dubbed them "McFilthy and McNasty," labeling them the dirtiest players he had ever seen. The Bullets' frontcourt duo ignored the criticisms, though, leading Washington to respectable 42–40 and 35–47 records in 1982–83 and 1983–84. "There were a lot of people out there that didn't like us, but Jeff and I didn't care," Mahorn later said. "We went out onto the court, and we played hard because we

Rick Mahorn was known for his physical play, ranking second in the NBA in personal fouls for three straight seasons in the early '80s.

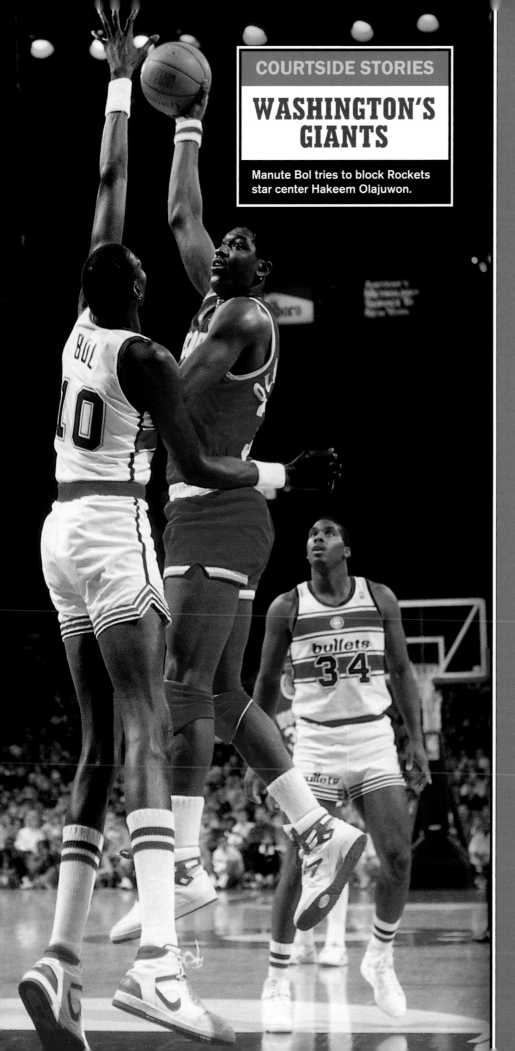

WASHINGTON'S GIANTS

Manute Bol tries to block Rockets star center Hakeem Olajuwon.

THE 1985–86 WASHINGTON BULLETS WERE NOT THE BEST TEAM OF ALL TIME, BUT THEY WERE ONE OF THE BIGGEST. Few NBA teams have ever sent a taller front line onto the court than the Bullets did when they put 6-foot-9 Cliff Robinson, 6-foot-11 Jeff Ruland, and 7-foot-6 Manute Bol in the lineup at the same time. Great height did not translate into great success, though, as Washington finished the season 39–43 and fell to Philadelphia in the first round of the playoffs. Surprisingly, despite their length, the Bullets did not even win the battle of the boards that season, as they were out-rebounded by more than 350 boards over the course of the season. Robinson, who had a reputation as a journeyman player, enjoyed a great season, averaging 18.7 points and 8.7 rebounds per game. Ruland was even better, pulling his weight with averages of 19 points and 10.7 boards per game. The weak rebounding link was the poor-jumping Bol, who snared only six rebounds per game—a figure that actually represented his career best.

JEFF MALONE WAS ONE OF THE MOST UNHER-
ALDED OF THE NBA'S GREAT SCORERS. After being
drafted by the Bullets in 1983 out of Mississippi State
University, he quietly proved to be an outstanding
shooter who could fill up the nets. Malone had a sig-
nature moment in his rookie season. In a game against
the Detroit Pistons, he heaved a last-second three-point

shot toward the basket as he fell backwards along the
baseline and flew out of bounds. The ball sailed over
the top of the backboard and swished in for the game-
winner. (Years later, fan voting on NBA.com would
name that shot 1 of the 10 best in NBA history.) Malone
averaged better than 20 points per game during 5 of
his 7 seasons with the Bullets and was a sensational

free-throw shooter, connecting on 86.9 percent of his
shots from the "charity stripe." "I didn't have to have the
ball in the last two minutes [of games]," the confident
Malone later said. "But if I did, I was going to make the
best of it."

A KING-SIZED COMEBACK

Bernard King levels a defender.

WHEN THE BULLETS SIGNED FREE-AGENT FORWARD BERNARD KING PRIOR TO THE 1987–88 SEASON, THE MOVE PROMPTED QUITE A FEW RAISED EYEBROWS AROUND THE NBA. King had been a star with the Knicks, but he had suffered a gruesome knee injury that caused him to miss the entire 1985–86 season, and he played only a handful of games the following year. The Knicks finally felt they had no other choice but to cut him from the roster, and the Bullets, who were struggling offensively at the time, decided they had nothing to lose by giving him a chance. King came through in a big way. He averaged 17.2 points a game with the Bullets in his first season, scoring 52 points against the Denver Nuggets in 1 game. He was even better in each of the next 3 seasons, reaching his peak in 1990–91, when he capped his amazing story by averaging 28.4 points per game. "To come back after the entire knee was reconstructed," King said, "is something that I'm awfully proud of."

were going to do anything we could to win. We were not dirty, and we did

not try to injure anyone. But we were trying to win, and we have nothing

to apologize for about the way we played."

A few seasons later, the Bullets featured one of the most interesting

teammate combinations in NBA history. In 1987–88, they put 7-foot-

6 center Manute Bol on the court at the same time as 5-foot-3 point

guard Tyrone "Muggsy" Bogues. Bol was a rail-thin shot-blocking special-

ist from Sudan who developed an awkward-looking but accurate three-

point shot, while the pint-sized Bogues used his speed and quickness to

energize Washington's offense and create scoring opportunities for such

talented teammates as guard Jeff Malone, center Moses Malone, and

forward Bernard King. The crowds in the Capital Centre adopted both

Bol and Bogues as fan favorites, and they cheered even louder as the

Bullets went 38–44 in 1987–88 and made the playoffs.

After falling to the Pistons in the 1988 playoffs, the Bullets would not

make the postseason again for nearly a decade. Still, Washington was

not devoid of talent. Former star Wes Unseld had been hired as head

coach in 1987, and he looked to Jeff Malone and King for steady scor-

ing. Malone was a brilliant shooter with a quick release, while King was

a former scorer extraordinaire with the Knicks who worked his way back to star status in Washington after suffering a devastating knee injury. "It was just a magnificent comeback," said Hubie Brown, who coached King in New York. "It seemed like he would not be able to come back from the injury, but he did it because he never accepted that he wouldn't be able to play anymore, and he did all the hard work he needed to do."

Still, the Bullets struggled for wins. Their defense was often porous, they struggled away from home, and they seemed to lack the "killer instinct" necessary to close out games in the fourth quarter. Unseld coached the team through 1994 and was then replaced by Jim Lynam. Washington finally earned a playoff berth again in 1997 after assembling an improved 44–38 record. By then, the Bullets featured a new lineup that included 7-foot-7 center Gheorghe Muresan, brawny forwards Chris Webber and Juwan Howard, and deft-passing guard Rod Strickland. Facing star guard Michael Jordan and the high-powered Chicago Bulls in the postseason, though, the Bullets were quickly swept aside.

A bruiser with a soft shooting touch, Chris Webber averaged better than 20 points per game in each of his 4 Washington seasons.

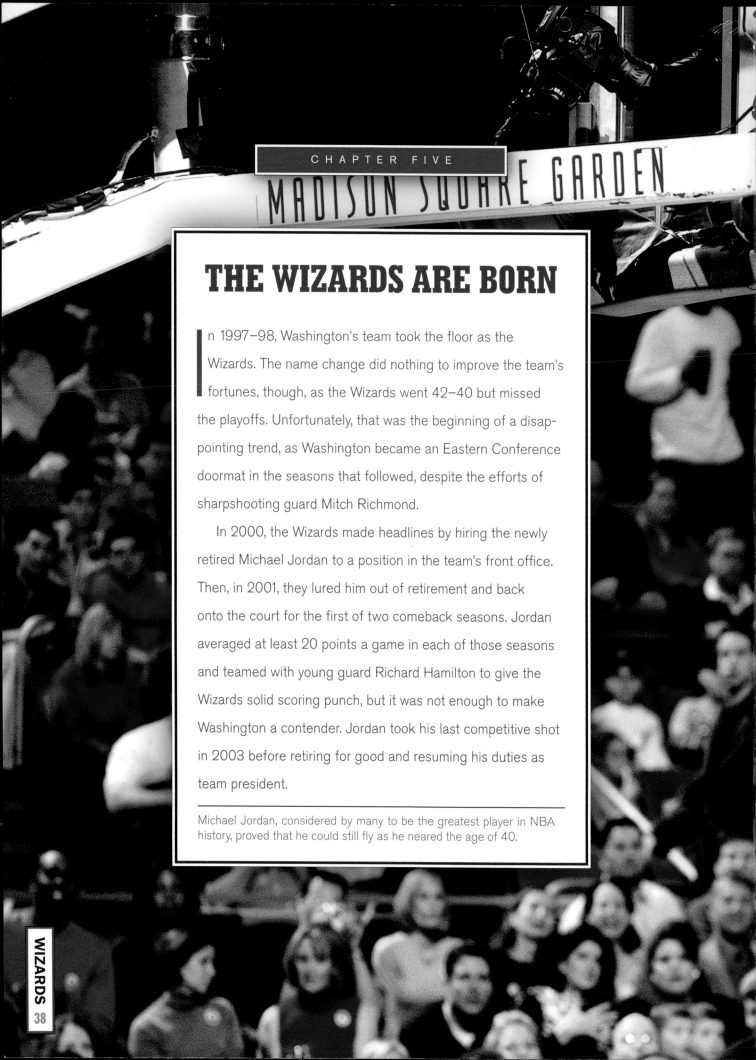

CHAPTER FIVE

THE WIZARDS ARE BORN

In 1997–98, Washington's team took the floor as the Wizards. The name change did nothing to improve the team's fortunes, though, as the Wizards went 42–40 but missed the playoffs. Unfortunately, that was the beginning of a disappointing trend, as Washington became an Eastern Conference doormat in the seasons that followed, despite the efforts of sharpshooting guard Mitch Richmond.

In 2000, the Wizards made headlines by hiring the newly retired Michael Jordan to a position in the team's front office. Then, in 2001, they lured him out of retirement and back onto the court for the first of two comeback seasons. Jordan averaged at least 20 points a game in each of those seasons and teamed with young guard Richard Hamilton to give the Wizards solid scoring punch, but it was not enough to make Washington a contender. Jordan took his last competitive shot in 2003 before retiring for good and resuming his duties as team president.

Michael Jordan, considered by many to be the greatest player in NBA history, proved that he could still fly as he neared the age of 40.

The 2004–05 season marked the start of a new era in Washington. The Wizards emerged as one of the most improved teams in the league behind three rising stars—guard Gilbert Arenas, forward Antawn Jamison, and swingman Larry Hughes. The trio averaged a combined 67.1 points per game and displayed an offensive versatility that made Washington one of the most difficult teams in the NBA to defend. Arenas keyed the attack with his confident outside shooting and creativity, Jamison flexed his muscle as an inside scoring force, and the lanky Hughes aggravated opposing defenses with his speed and ability to play multiple positions. The Bullets rolled to a 45–37 record and won their first best-of-seven playoff series since 1979 when they rallied to beat the Bulls in six games.

Even though the Bullets lost to the Miami Heat in the second round of the playoffs, the team's new youth movement had many Washington fans—and players—thinking big. "We have the kind of team that can win a lot of games together," said Arenas. "We all like each other, and we all want to play for each other. When we played the Bulls in the playoffs, none of us had any sense of panic because we lost the first two games.... We figured if we could play our regular game once we got home, that was all we needed to do. That's just how it worked out for us."

in you?

COURTSIDE STORIES

ENDING THE DROUGHT

Larry Hughes rises above Bulls defenders in the 2005 playoffs.

OVER THE COURSE OF THEIR HISTORY, THE WIZARDS HAVE ENDURED THEIR SHARE OF SLUMPS. As the Bullets, they won the 1978 NBA championship, then lost in the NBA Finals the following year. That defeat marked the end of the franchise's run as a perennial playoff power. The Bullets made the postseason in seven of the following nine seasons but earned only one series victory, in 1982. After losing to the Pistons in the first round of the 1988 playoffs, the franchise would not make another playoff appearance until 1997, when it was swept by the Bulls. The team then went into another funk, not partaking in the postseason again until 2005, when it met Chicago again. This time, the Wizards finally ended the drought. Although Washington dropped the first two games, tough team defense and the offensive exploits of star guard Gilbert Arenas propelled the Wizards to the series victory. "We thought we were the better team," Arenas said. "But after we lost the first two games, we realized we had to go out and prove it every minute. We turned it up a couple of notches."

INTRODUCING...

ANTAWN JAMISON

POSITION FORWARD
HEIGHT 6-FOOT-8
WIZARDS SEASONS 2004–10

ANTAWN JAMISON WON THE NATIONAL COLLEGE PLAYER OF THE YEAR AWARD IN 1998 WHILE PLAYING FOR THE POWERHOUSE UNIVERSITY OF NORTH CAROLINA. During his first 5 NBA seasons playing for the Golden State Warriors, he twice scored 51 points in a game. When he was traded to the Wizards in 2004, he maintained the consistently high level of play he had established during his Golden State years. In 10 of the 11 seasons from 1999–2000 to 2009–10, he never averaged fewer than 18.7 points and 6.8 boards per game. Yet Jamison was somewhat overlooked as a star in Washington, due largely to the fact that he lacked the outgoing personality of such teammates as Gilbert Arenas. Few players in the game, though, were as universally liked and respected as Jamison. "You're not going to meet a nicer guy than him," said Garry St. Jean, who coached Jamison when he was with the Warriors. "If you told me, in my 26 years [in the NBA], to pick my 5 best people' players, he'd be one of them." During the 2009–10 season, Jamison was traded to Cleveland.

A HISTORY OF NAMES

G-Wiz, Washington's mascot.

THE WASHINGTON WIZARDS FRANCHISE HAS UNDERGONE MORE NAME CHANGES THAN ANY OTHER PROFESSIONAL SPORTS TEAM. They were born in Chicago as an expansion team called the Packers (in reference to the city's meat-packing industry) in 1961. A year later, new ownership changed the team's name to the Zephyrs (a reference to a Greek wind god—fitting for the "Windy City" of Chicago). Chicago basketball fans would eventually go wild for the Bulls, but they did not take to the Packers/Zephyrs. The club therefore moved to Baltimore in 1963, changing its name to the Bullets (after another NBA team that had played there in the 1940s and '50s). The Bullets moved to Washington in 1973, changing their name to the Capital Bullets. The next season, the team's name changed once again, to the Washington Bullets. By the 1990s, team owner Abe Pollin grew uncomfortable with the violent connotation of the name "Bullets." In 1997, as the club opened its new home, the MCI Center, he announced that the team would henceforth be known as the Wizards, a name that had been chosen above such other possibilities as the Monuments, Express, and Seadogs.

Unfortunately, Washington's promising core was reduced by one when Hughes left town in 2005, and the rest of the Wizards struggled to climb the Eastern Conference ladder. Arenas was plagued by injury problems, and although the Wizards made the playoffs in 2006, 2007, and 2008, they could never get past the first round. Washington fans found a new nemesis in star forward LeBron James, whose Cleveland Cavaliers knocked the Wizards from the postseason three years in a row.

The 2008–09 season was a dark one in the nation's capital, as Arenas missed virtually the entire season with a knee injury, and the Wizards limped to a 19–63 record, tied for worst in franchise history. The next year was not much better. First, longtime team owner Abe Pollin died early in the season. Then Arenas was suspended and criminally charged after he brought guns into the team's locker room. Shortly after that, Jamison and two other players were traded away, and the best player received in return, swingman Josh Howard, promptly suffered a knee injury. Even though young forward Andray Blatche stepped up his game, the Wizards went 26–56. "Next year's going to be better," Pollin's widow, Irene, told fans after the season. "I can promise you that."

The Wizards, a team with many names during its first half century

of existence, has both celebrated moments of glory and suffered

stretches of despair. Yet boasting an all-time roster that includes

such names as Earl "The Pearl" Monroe, Elvin Hayes, and Michael

Jordan, Washington's franchise—win or lose—has rarely been boring.

With a touch of luck, the day may soon come when America's capital is

once again the capital of the basketball world.

Guard Randy Foye (opposite) left Washington in 2010, leaving Andray
Blatche (below) and rookie guard John Wall to lead the Wizards.

INDEX